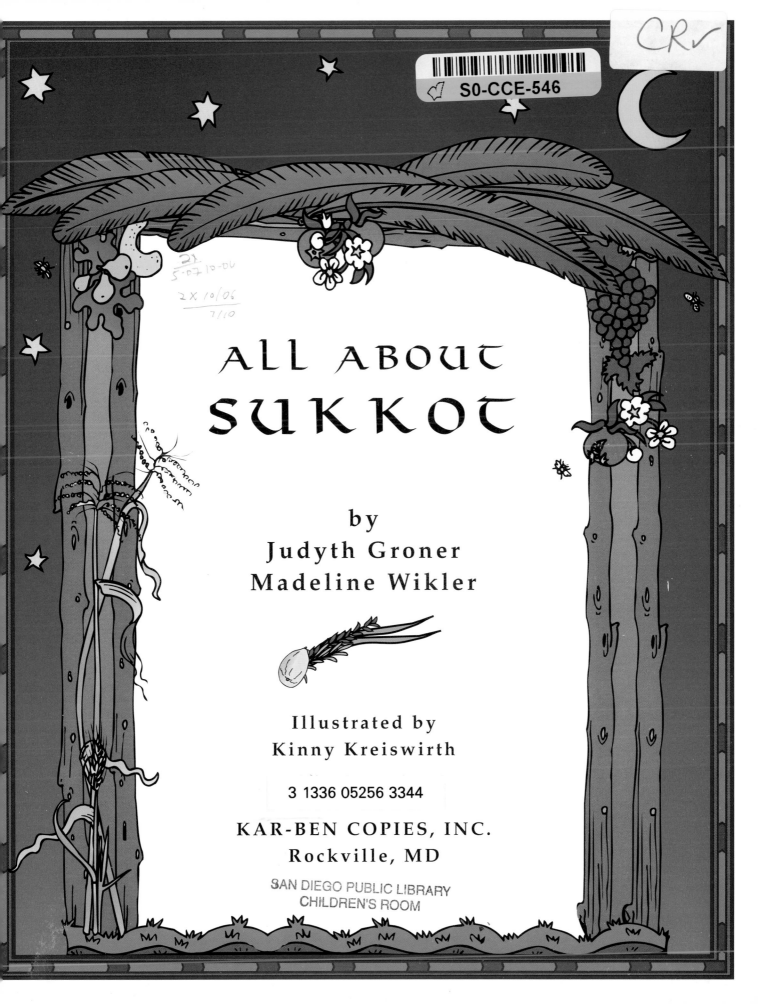

ALL ABOUT
SUKKOT

by
Judyth Groner
Madeline Wikler

Illustrated by
Kinny Kreiswirth

KAR-BEN COPIES, INC.
Rockville, MD

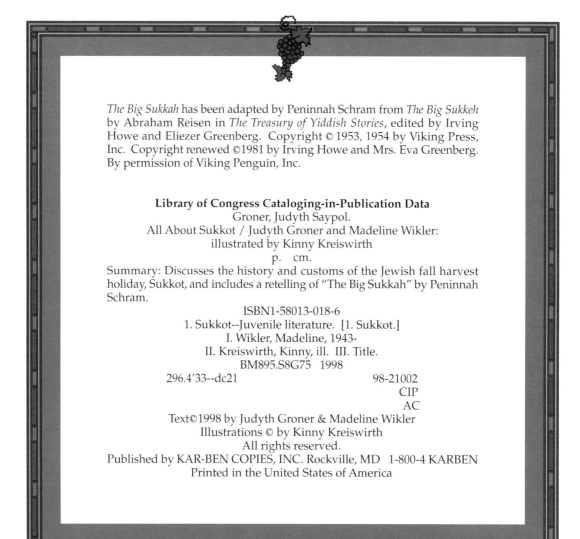

The Big Sukkah has been adapted by Peninnah Schram from *The Big Sukkeh* by Abraham Reisen in *The Treasury of Yiddish Stories*, edited by Irving Howe and Eliezer Greenberg. Copyright © 1953, 1954 by Viking Press, Inc. Copyright renewed ©1981 by Irving Howe and Mrs. Eva Greenberg. By permission of Viking Penguin, Inc.

Library of Congress Cataloging-in-Publication Data
Groner, Judyth Saypol.
All About Sukkot / Judyth Groner and Madeline Wikler:
illustrated by Kinny Kreiswirth
p.   cm.
Summary: Discusses the history and customs of the Jewish fall harvest holiday, Sukkot, and includes a retelling of "The Big Sukkah" by Peninnah Schram.
ISBN1-58013-018-6
1. Sukkot--Juvenile literature. [1. Sukkot.]
I. Wikler, Madeline, 1943-
II. Kreiswirth, Kinny, ill. III. Title.
BM895.S8G75 1998
296.4'33--dc21   98-21002
                                                                  CIP
                                                                  AC
Text©1998 by Judyth Groner & Madeline Wikler
Illustrations © by Kinny Kreiswirth
All rights reserved.
Published by KAR-BEN COPIES, INC. Rockville, MD 1-800-4 KARBEN
Printed in the United States of America

For everything there is a season.

For everything there is a time.
A time to weep and a time to laugh.
A time to keep silent and a time to speak.
A time to plant and a time to harvest.

Summer is over. Farmers have gathered the crops from the fields. Leaves are changing color and falling from the trees. The days are getting shorter.

The time of Sukkot has come.
Sukkot celebrates the season of the harvest.

סוכות

The Festival of the Harvest

Long ago, Jewish people were shepherds and farmers. During the growing season, they went out to work in the fields and came home to their villages at night.

But during the harvest, the fruits and vegetables were ripe and would spoil if not picked quickly. There was no time for the farmers to return to their villages, so they built huts out in the fields for shelter and rest.

When the harvest was finished, the farmers returned home and celebrated. They were thankful that they would have enough food for the long winter ahead.

*Building a sukkah
is a celebration of nature.*

THE FESTIVAL OF BOOTHS

Holidays help us to remember important times in the long history of the Jewish people. On Passover, we tell the story of how the Jewish slaves were freed. On Shavuot, we recall the giving of the Torah on Mount Sinai.

On Sukkot, we remember that after leaving Egypt, the Jews wandered in the desert for 40 years. When they were tired, they built huts (sukkot) for shade and rest. The huts were not very big and not very comfortable.

But the people shared a dream that soon they would reach a land with rivers, trees, and fruit...a land where they would be free...a land where they could build homes for protection.

Building a sukkah
reminds us of our history.

A TIME OF GLADNESS

Long ago, Jews from all over the world traveled to Jerusalem to celebrate holidays at the Holy Temple. The travelers were called pilgrims, and their journey was called a pilgrimage. Sukkot was a favorite time for such a trip, because the harvest was over.

Thousands came. Rich Jews drove chariots, others rode donkeys and camels. Some came by boat; others traveled on foot. They spoke many languages and had different customs, but they shared a common history and faith.

Streets were decorated with fruits and branches. For shelter, the pilgrims built sukkot (huts) in courtyards and on rooftops. There were parades and dances, sacrifices and feasts.

*Building a sukkah
reminds us of the pilgrimage to Jerusalem.*

The Water-Drawing Ceremony

The rabbis said that on Sukkot, God decides how much rain will fall during the coming year.

In Israel, the summer is completely dry. Fall and winter rains prepare the earth for spring planting. If there is no rain, there will be no crops, and people will go hungry.

During the Sukkot celebration at the Holy Temple, a special rain ceremony was held. People marched to a nearby spring and drew water in golden pitchers. Lamps were lit in the courtyard, the shofar was blown, and the water was poured on the Temple altar. People sang and danced to the music of trumpets, harps and cymbals.

SUKKOT TODAY

We no longer make a pilgrimage to the Holy Temple, but we continue to celebrate Sukkot at home and in the synagogue.

Many families build sukkot and eat their meals there. They may also study and read in the sukkah and even sleep there on warm nights. Those who don't build sukkot may decorate their homes with fruit and branches, or make tabletop sukkot to use as centerpieces for holiday meals.

The synagogue is a festive place on Sukkot. The rabbi, cantor, and members of the congregation parade around the bimah and down the aisles carrying the lulav and etrog and singing prayers of thanksgiving. After services everyone gathers in the sukkah for kiddush and refreshments.

It has become a custom to invite Biblical heroes to join us in the sukkah each night. They are called ushpizin, guests. We invite Abraham, Isaac, Jacob, Joseph, Moses, Aaron, and David. Some families also invite women of the Bible, such as Sarah, Rachel, Rebecca, Leah, Miriam, Deborah, and Hannah. You can make or buy decorative posters of the ushpizin and read or tell stories about them during holiday meals.

Each morning, except for Shabbat, a blessing is recited over the lulav and etrog. When Jews lived in the villages of Eastern Europe they imported these crops from Israel or another warm land. Most families could not afford to buy their own and had to share. Children would carry the lulav and etrog from house to house so everyone could recite the blessing. After Sukkot, they would make the rounds again - to collect payment.

the sukkah

he Torah tells us:

You shall live in huts seven days in order that future generations may know that I made the Israelites live in huts when I brought them out of Egypt.

The sukkah also reminds us of huts the Israelite farmers built in the fields during the harvest, and shelters the Jews built in Jerusalem during their pilgrimage to the Holy Temple.

The sukkah is not strong. It shakes in the wind and rain. It reminds us that even though we live in sturdy homes, not all families live in peace, comfort, and safety.

There are only a few rules to follow in building a sukkah. The rest is up to your imagination.

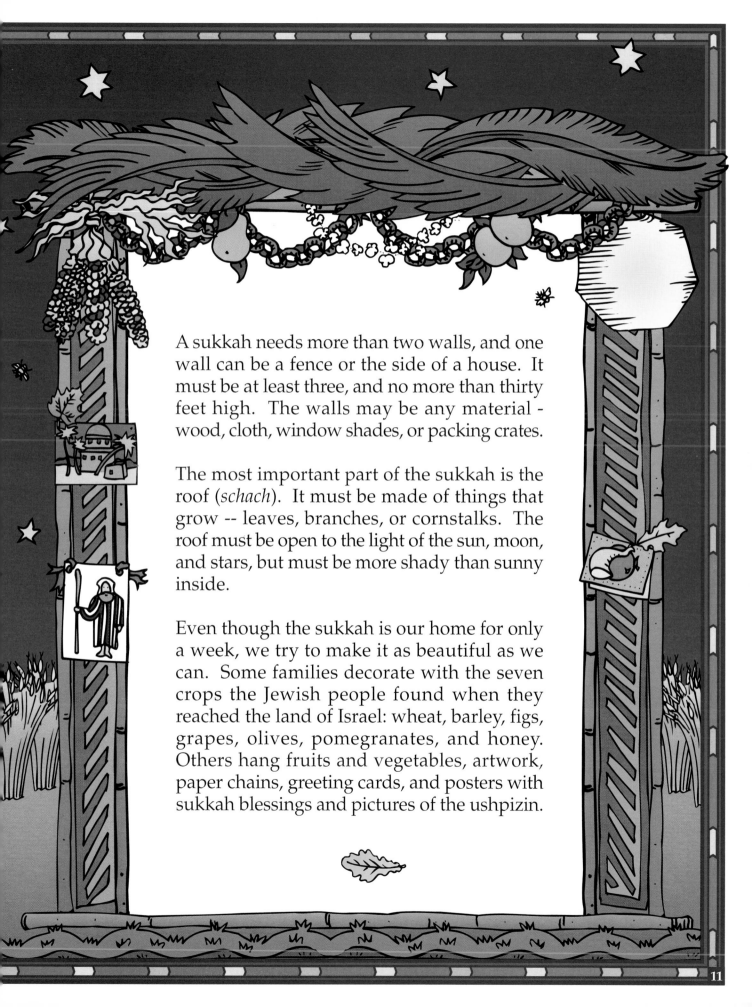

A sukkah needs more than two walls, and one wall can be a fence or the side of a house. It must be at least three, and no more than thirty feet high. The walls may be any material - wood, cloth, window shades, or packing crates.

The most important part of the sukkah is the roof (*schach*). It must be made of things that grow -- leaves, branches, or cornstalks. The roof must be open to the light of the sun, moon, and stars, but must be more shady than sunny inside.

Even though the sukkah is our home for only a week, we try to make it as beautiful as we can. Some families decorate with the seven crops the Jewish people found when they reached the land of Israel: wheat, barley, figs, grapes, olives, pomegranates, and honey. Others hang fruits and vegetables, artwork, paper chains, greeting cards, and posters with sukkah blessings and pictures of the ushpizin.

LULAV & ETROG

he Torah tells us -

When you have gathered in the harvest crops, you shall celebrate. You shall take the branches and fruit of beautiful trees and you shall rejoice.

The branches and fruit that we use are:

LULAV - the branch of a palm tree
HADASIM - three boughs of a leafy myrtle
ARAVOT - two branches of a willow tree
ETROG - the lemon-like fruit of a citron

We hold them together, recite a blessing, and shake them in all directions to show that God is everywhere.

The lulav and etrog stand for the crops of the harvest, but tradition has given them additional meanings.

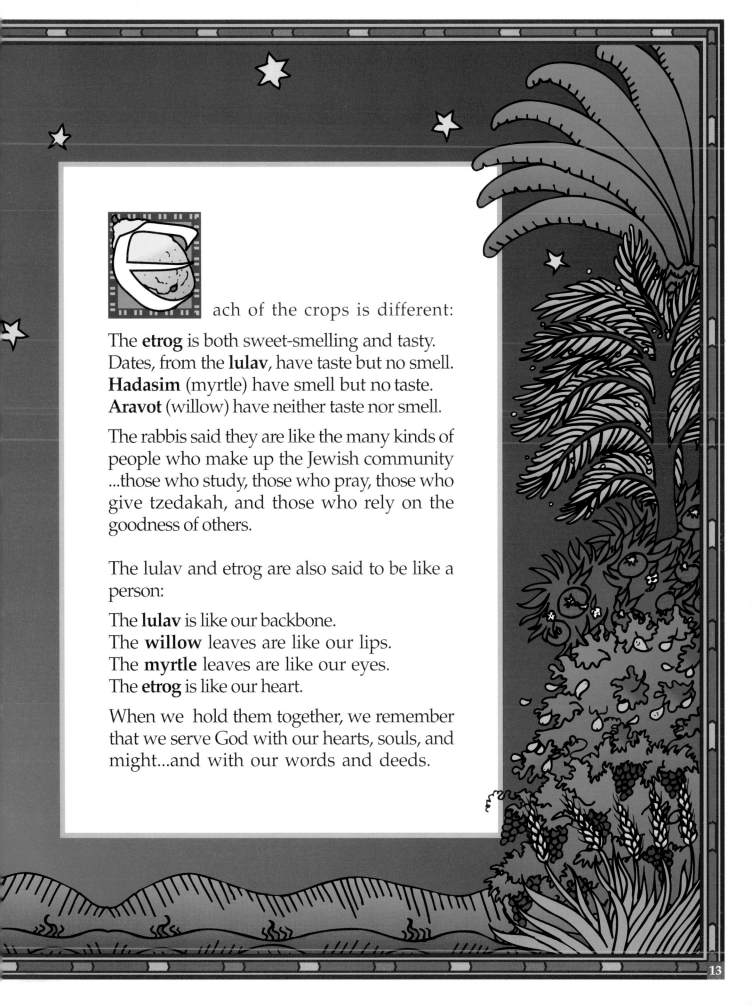

ach of the crops is different:

The **etrog** is both sweet-smelling and tasty.
Dates, from the **lulav**, have taste but no smell.
Hadasim (myrtle) have smell but no taste.
Aravot (willow) have neither taste nor smell.

The rabbis said they are like the many kinds of people who make up the Jewish community ...those who study, those who pray, those who give tzedakah, and those who rely on the goodness of others.

The lulav and etrog are also said to be like a person:

The **lulav** is like our backbone.
The **willow** leaves are like our lips.
The **myrtle** leaves are like our eyes.
The **etrog** is like our heart.

When we hold them together, we remember that we serve God with our hearts, souls, and might...and with our words and deeds.

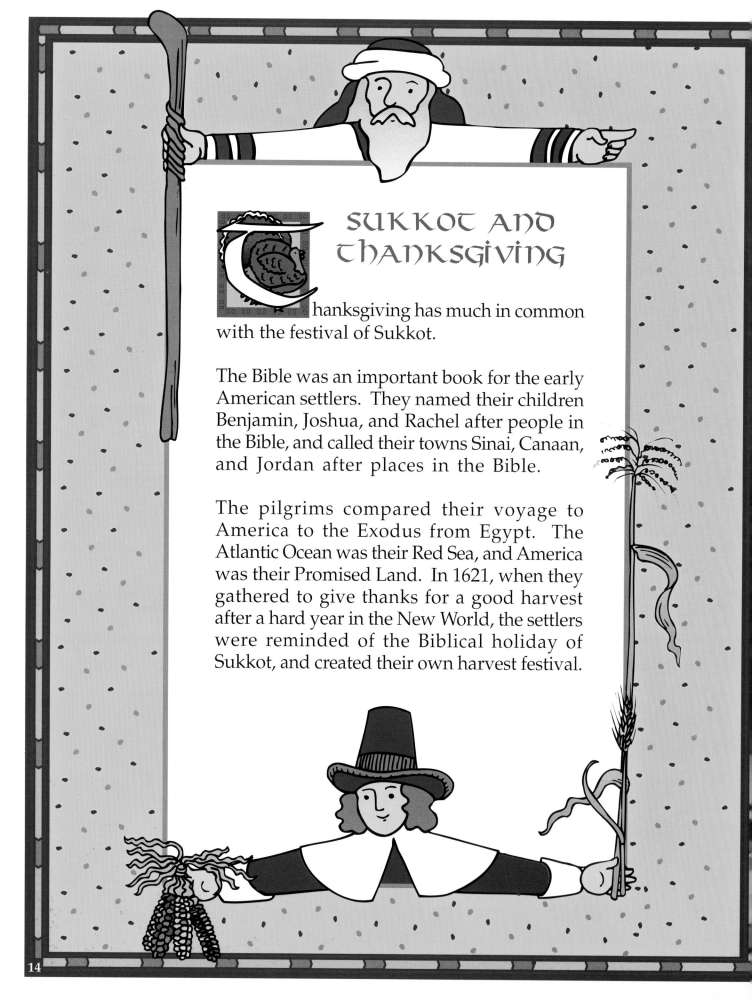

SUKKOT AND THANKSGIVING

Thanksgiving has much in common with the festival of Sukkot.

The Bible was an important book for the early American settlers. They named their children Benjamin, Joshua, and Rachel after people in the Bible, and called their towns Sinai, Canaan, and Jordan after places in the Bible.

The pilgrims compared their voyage to America to the Exodus from Egypt. The Atlantic Ocean was their Red Sea, and America was their Promised Land. In 1621, when they gathered to give thanks for a good harvest after a hard year in the New World, the settlers were reminded of the Biblical holiday of Sukkot, and created their own harvest festival.

SUKKOT IN ISRAEL

On many of Israel's kibbutzim, agriculture is an important industry, and the harvest celebration is a joyous festival. Members build huge sukkot, large enough for all the families, and decorate them with fruits and vegetables grown on their farms.

Israel depends on winter rains, and there are music and dance festivals to recall the water-drawing ceremony at the Holy Temple. Families take hiking and camping trips to enjoy the fall weather.

Throughout the week, in cities and towns, you can see people - young and old - walking to synagogues with their lulav and etrog, and enjoying festive meals in sukkot built on rooftops and balconies, even on sidewalks in front of restaurants.

SHEMINI ATZERET

A king once invited friends to his palace for a great feast. When the guests prepared to leave, the king said, "Please stay with me one more day. It is hard for me to say good-bye."

Sukkot, too, is a joyous festival, and we would like it to last one more day. So we celebrate Shemini Atzeret, the Eighth Day of Gathering, as a closing holiday. In the synagogue we offer prayers to remember family and friends who have died. We also recite a beautiful prayer for rain:

Dear God,
Who causes the wind to blow and the rain to fall,
Bring us the blessing of gentle showers.
Crown the valleys with green fruits.
Cool the dried earth with life-giving rain.

THE BIG SUKKAH

retold by Peninnah Schram

In the village of Lepel, in a very small cottage, lived a very large family. There were the parents, Berel and Rivke, and their six children, Motel, Reyzel, Yankel, Malke, Esther, and Shmuel.

A very large cupboard separated the cottage into a front part and a back part. In the back were the beds. In the front stood an enormous stove and a long table with some wooden benches.

Berel and Rivke had many relatives. Whenever there was a holiday they could never invite them to their house, because there was not enough space. "What kind of celebration would it be with everyone bumping into each other," Berel and Rivke said to each other.

Instead, on every holiday the relatives, especially wealthy Uncle Avrom, would invite Berel, Rivke, and the children to their homes for a feast. Berel and Rivke accepted these generous invitations, but they always felt ashamed that they could not return the hospitality.

Year after year, Berel would say to his hosts, "Next time, you come to us," and his voice would drift off.

One year, as soon as Yom Kippur was over, Motel and Shmuel helped their father bring the old wooden boards down from the attic, and Berel began to build his sukkah.

"Wait a minute!" he thought to himself, as he nailed the boards together. "It's true I have the smallest house in the village, but I have a very big yard. If I put these boards on the other side of the house, and if I connect the wall to my neighbor's wooden fence..."

Berel laughed with joy at this discovery.

He told Shmuel to fetch three storm windows from the attic, and sent Yankel and Motel to remove the two large doors from the kitchen cupboard.

When he was finished, Berel couldn't believe his eyes. It was the largest sukkah he had ever seen.

"Rivke," he called out with excitement. "Look how roomy! It's big enough for 100 people! Now we can invite the whole family, even the whole town, to our sukkah." He took her by the arm.

"We have no time to dance now," Rivke said. She called the children and gave each one a job.

Malke swept the ground and spread sand over it. Yankel and Shmuel carried the table and benches from the house. Reyzel and Esther brought the tablecloths, dishes, and silverware. Motel gathered pine branches for the roof.

Together they decorated with fresh fruit, wild flowers, and branches. The sukkah smelled sweet, and it was very beautiful.

On the first night of Sukkos, Berel and Rivke and the children gathered in the sukkah with the whole family: grandparents, uncles, aunts, nieces, and nephews.

Uncle Avrom turned to Berel, "This is such a large and wonderful sukkah! So many of us together at one time! And what delicious food! You know, my sukkah is such a tiny one that it's not possible to invite the whole family at once."

When Berel heard this, he beamed. Everyone nodded with approval.

From that time on, Berel and Rivke continued to enjoy the holidays at the homes of relatives. But they knew that on Sukkos, they would return the family's hospitality in their own, very big sukkah.

סוכות

HOME SERVICE FOR
SUKKOT

TZEDAKAh

Tzedakah was an important mitzvah for Jewish farmers, especially at the time of the harvest.

The Torah commands farmers to leave a portion of crops unpicked, so the poor might glean (gather) them for food.

Farmers also are required to set aside a tithe (a tenth) of their grain, oil, wine, and livestock. A portion was used to feed the priests at the Holy Temple, and a portion to feed the poor.

Today, some families help glean crops to donate to food banks. Others contribute funds to shelters and soup kitchens that help to feed the hungry.

ḤADLAKAT ṄEROT
CAṄDLE-LightiṄG

We welcome Sukkot with the lighting of the candles:

בָּרוּךְ אַתָּה יְיָ אֱלֹהֵינוּ מֶלֶךְ הָעוֹלָם,
אֲשֶׁר קִדְּשָׁנוּ בְּמִצְוֹתָיו וְצִוָּנוּ
לְהַדְלִיק נֵר שֶׁל (שַׁבָּת וְשֶׁל) יוֹם טוֹב.

Baruch Atah Adonai Eloheinu Melech ha'olam,
Asher kid'shanu b'mitzvotav v'tzivanu
L'hadlik ner shel (Shabbat v'shel) Yom Tov.

בָּרוּךְ אַתָּה יְיָ אֱלֹהֵינוּ מֶלֶךְ הָעוֹלָם,
שֶׁהֶחֱיָנוּ וְקִיְּמָנוּ וְהִגִּיעָנוּ לַזְּמַן הַזֶּה.

Baruch Atah Adonai Eloheinu Melech ha'olam,
Shehecheyanu, vekiy'manu v'higiyanu laz'man hazeh.

Thank you, God, for bringing us together to celebrate Sukkot, and for the mitzvah of lighting the candles.

As the glow of the moon and stars brings light to our Sukkah, may these candles shine upon us in joy and in peace.

KIDDUSH
BLESSING OVER WINE

The Kiddush proclaims the holiness of Sukkot.

בָּרוּךְ אַתָּה יְיָ אֱלֹהֵינוּ מֶלֶךְ הָעוֹלָם, בּוֹרֵא פְּרִי הַגָּפֶן.

Baruch Atah Adonai Eloheinu Melech ha'olam, borei p'ri hagafen.

Thank You, God, for the blessing of wine. We recall the history of our people, and rejoice in the harvest.

בָּרוּךְ אַתָּה יְיָ אֱלֹהֵינוּ מֶלֶךְ הָעוֹלָם,
אֲשֶׁר קִדְּשָׁנוּ בְּמִצְוֹתָיו וְצִוָּנוּ לֵישֵׁב בַּסֻּכָּה.

Baruch Atah Adonai Eloheinu Melech ha'olam,
Asher kid'shanu b'mitzvotav v'tzivanu leshev basukkah.

בָּרוּךְ אַתָּה יְיָ אֱלֹהֵינוּ מֶלֶךְ הָעוֹלָם,
שֶׁהֶחֱיָנוּ וְקִיְּמָנוּ וְהִגִּיעָנוּ לַזְּמַן הַזֶּה.

Baruch Atah Adonai Eloheinu Melech ha'olam,
Shehecheyanu, vekiy'manu v'higiyanu laz'man hazeh.

Thank You, God, for the mitzvah of dwelling in the sukkah, and for bringing our family and friends together to celebrate this festival.

HAMOTZI
CHALLAH BLESSING

As we enjoy our challah we are grateful for the bounty of the harvest.

בָּרוּךְ אַתָּה יְיָ אֱלֹהֵינוּ מֶלֶךְ הָעוֹלָם,
הַמּוֹצִיא לֶחֶם מִן הָאָרֶץ.

Baruch Atah Adonai Eloheinu Melech ha'olam,
Hamotzi lechem min ha'aretz.

Thank You, God, for the blessing of bread and for the festive meal which we will now enjoy together.

USHPIZIN

Enter, honored, holy guest* and be seated. As we welcome you to our sukkah, we recall your life, and remember the good deeds of the generations of men and women who came before us.

*Abraham, Isaac, Jacob, Joseph, Moses, David, Aaron
Sarah, Rebecca, Rachel, Leah, Miriam, Deborah, Hannah

BLESSING FOR SUKKOT

Each morning during Sukkot, except for Shabbat, we recite a blessing over the lulav and etrog.

Hold the lulav in your right hand and the etrog in your left hand. The stem of the etrog should be pointing up, and the lulav and etrog should be touching.

בָּרוּךְ אַתָּה יְיָ אֱלֹהֵינוּ מֶלֶךְ הָעוֹלָם,
אֲשֶׁר קִדְּשָׁנוּ בְּמִצְוֹתָיו וְצִוָּנוּ עַל נְטִילַת לוּלַב.

Baruch Atah Adonai Eloheinu Melech ha'olam,
Asher kid'shanu b'mitzvotav v'tzivanu al n'tilat lulav.

Thank You, God, for these fragrant fruits of the harvest, for the sun and rain which make them grow, for the seasons of nature and the seasons of our lives.

After the blessing, turn the etrog so the stem is pointing down. Wave the lulav and etrog together in all directions-- north, south, east, west, up, and down.

BİRKAT HAMAZON
AFTER THE MEAL

We join in giving thanks for the festive meal we have eaten.

בָּרוּךְ אַתָּה יְיָ, הַזָּן אֶת-הַכֹּל.

Baruch Atah Adonai, hazan et hakol.

עֹשֶׂה שָׁלוֹם בִּמְרוֹמָיו הוּא יַעֲשֶׂה שָׁלוֹם
עָלֵינוּ וְעַל כָּל-יִשְׂרָאֵל. וְאִמְרוּ אָמֵן.

Oseh shalom bimromav hu ya'aseh shalom
Aleinu v'al kol Yisrael. Ve'imru amen.

Thank You, God,
for the festive meal we have shared,
for the food we have eaten at this table,
for the Torah and mitzvot which guide our lives,
for Israel, the homeland of the Jewish people,
for our freedom to live as Jews,
for life, strength, and health.
Bless our family, and grant us a good year.

LIGHTING THE CANDLES

*Freely adapted after a version
by A.W. BINDER*

Freely, as a chant

Ba - ruch a - tah a - do nai e - lo - hei - nu me - lech ha-

o - lam, a - sher kid - sha - nu b'mitz - vo - tav v'tzi - va - nu l' - had - lik

ner, l' had - lik ner, shel Yom - tov.

SHEHECHEYANU

Traditional

Ba - ruch a - tah a - do - nai e - lo - hei - nu me - lech ha - o - lam she -

he - che - ya - nu v' - kiy' - ma - nu v' - hi - gi - ya - nu la - z'man ha - zeh.

LESHEV BASUKKAH

TRADITIONAL

Ba - ruch a - tah a - do - nai e - lo - hei - nu me - lech hao - lam_____

a - sher kid - sha - nu b' - mitz - vo - tav v' - tzi - va - nu le - shev ba - suk - kah._____

KIDDUSH

TRADITIONAL

BIRKAT HAMAZON

M. NATHANSON

Flowing, in a thankful manner

Ba - ruch a - tah ___ a - do - nai e - lo -

hei - nu me-lech ha-o - lam ha - zan et ha-o - lam ku - lo b'-tu-vo b'-

chen b'- che - sed uv' ra - cha-mim hu no - ten le - chem l'chol ba - sar

ki l' - o - lam chas - do uv' - tu - vo ha - ga - dol ta -

mid lo cha-sar la-nu v'- al yech-sar la-nu ma - zon l'-o - lam va - ed ba-a -

vur sh'-mo ha-ga-dol _____ ki hu el zan um'-far-nes la - kol u-mei -

tiv la - kol u-mei-chin ma - zon l' - chol b'ri-o-tav a - sher ___ ba - ra. Ba -

ruch a - tah ___ a - do - nai _____ ha-zan ___ et ha - kol.

I'M BUILDING A SUKKAH

FOLK

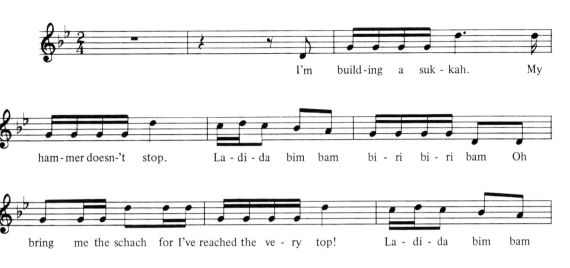

I'm build-ing a suk-kah. My ham-mer doesn-'t stop. La - di - da bim bam bi - ri bi - ri bam Oh bring me the schach for I've reached the ve - ry top! La - di - da bim bam bi - ri bi - ri bam, La - di - da bim bam bi - ri bi - ri bam.

2. I'll sit in the Sukkah like Noah in the Ark.
   La-di-da, . . .
   I'll drink and be merry from morning to dark!
   La-di-da, . . .

3. Come friends and neighbors, come right along.
   La-di-da, . . .
   Join us in eating and singing a song.
   La-di-da. . . .

Add your own verses!

P E R O T
(Fruit)

FOLK

Pe - rot, pe - rot. Who wants to buy pe -rot? Pe - rot for Suk-kot. Ap - ples grapes and or - an - ges, ap - ples grapes and or - an - ges. a to-ma - to on the roof Pe - rot for Suk - kot.

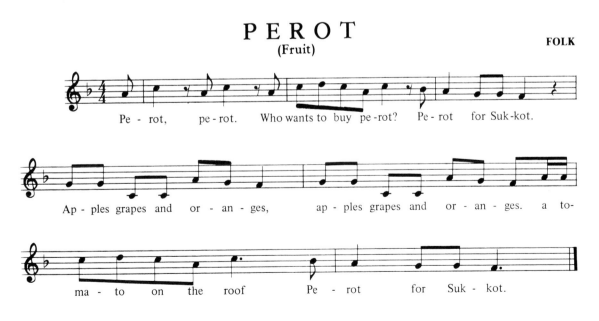

Perot, perot.
Mi rotzeh liknot.
Perot lechag Sukkot.
Anavim vetapuchim (2)
Ve'agvaniah
Lit lot al gag sukkah.

LAMA SUKKAH ZU?

CHASIDIC MELODY

La - mah suk - kah zu, A - ba tov she -

1 li? 2 li. Le - shev ba - suk - kah ya - ki - ri, Le -

shev ba - suk - kah cha - vi - vi, Le - shev ba - suk - kah

ye - led chen - ye - led chen she - li.

2. Lamah leshev bah, aba tov sheli?
   Avotenu yakiri,
   Avotenu chavivi,
   Avotenu af gam hemah
   Yashvu basukkah.

VESAMACHTA

FOLK

Ve - sa - mach - ta be - cha - ge - cha ve - ha - yi - ta

ach sa - me - ach ach - ach - ach sa - me - ach ach.

Ve - sa - mach - ta be - cha - ge - cha ve - ha - yi - ta

ach sa - me - ach ach - ach - sa - me - ach ach.